D. MARS YUVARAJAN

WILD.

POEMS

PROPHET.

WORKS OF MARS PRESS

Other Works by the Author

Night Owl and Other Poems

. M .oments (Volume One)

. M .oments (Volume Two)

Quiet Songs From Yesterday

Kintsugi

We Live With the Departed

In My Dreams, I Walk Through Killing Fields

Paradise of Weeping Hearts

These Untethered Affections

I Regret Only Everything

D. MARS YUVARAJAN

WILD.
PROPHET.

POEMS

WORKS OF MARS PRESS

ARS POËTICA FONS VÊRITÂTÈS EST

First edition published in 2019 by
WORKS OF MARS PRESS LIMITED
Auckland
New Zealand
www.worksofmars.com

ISBN: 978-0-9951008-7-9

A catalogue record for this book is available from the National Library of New Zealand.
Kei te pātengi raraunga o Te Puna Mātauranga o Aotearoa te whakarārangi o tēnei pukapuka.

For information about special discounts available for bulk purchases, sales promotions, fund-raising and educational needs, contact WORKS OF MARS PRESS LIMITED at (001) 603-443-2821 or worksofmars@gmail.com

Contact the Author at: worksofmars@gmail.com

Front Cover, Design and Layout by Dushyandhan 'Mars' Yuvarajan

I met, once, a man who was very sad,
who cried for a daughter yet to be had,
And when said daughter was pried to life
Instead of broad joy he filled with strife
As she did not resemble his loving wife
But softly threw a gaze much like his own,
So that he knew his demons had been sown
Into her wet and innocent flesh.

Contents.

Prelude to Annihilation

When I die…let it be with my head in your lap—

        Provoked hands—with warrant—rifling through my hair

     At having, once again, settled as the stone weight upon your thighs

and the hinderance to your existence.

        And every fictive ire shall irrigate, then dissipate—every memory of

     petty squabble or worthless insult will be

Commanded to drift to atoms and be swept along the coasts of the world;

        some coming to sit and watch, forever, the Northern skies, and some to the
        South

     to be entrenched under the unprinted night.

All the moments of pleasure and contentment shall regurgitate in fleeting

     stills across the inner sheets of my eyes, with every second

     drawn to a day—remembering the sweet running flesh of stone fruit—

one bite transferring incalculable movements—one fruit to an eternity.

        Where my stomach shall be consoled—full of sweet milk and jams; sweeter for
        the truth

     your palatial compassion has pursed within them. Macerating thick matter

with a surrender that no tart berry can claim as its own—and no herd can proffer.

        My skin effusing the fragrance of tortured seaweed and the brine of an inward
        tide

     shall gently anoint my fractional dreams along your seams.

Arms wiry and sinewed, from having planted every imaginable summer

     rapture, shall be unfurled upon your soft belly; its hairs a wild field upon
smooth sand.

§

Ears set to the volcanic gurgle of human entropy shall pick the faint

plucks of tendon, muscle, vein, and artery—sleep bagged with tumbling chaos.

And when I pass away quickly upon the legs that I have loved continuously—

it shall be as the mystics, contorted yet tranquil.

The unhindered respiratory hymn of my years shall eclipse languidly with the

mastered lethargy of biology, drifting to the dreams I have dreamt before.

When I die, let it be with my head in your lap—

My face unmasked. Eyes un-working, shall I wake within myself, and parting the final

temple door of seclusion will I find you there—no differently greeting me again.

i.

The walls ring hollow—
        with lame fingers, a brittle herd, riding
Upon the undulations of their waxy skin,
Which in some joyous seconds pierce
To the sweet honeycomb within;
        in contrast
To the concert of a flat dull silence, around.
Nothing, she sings—she, being the wind
Outside, and inside the hull is an audience
raptured to the whistling tune through the teeth
        of a gap toothed timber.
Attuned to the ruby throated hum
        and incessant whine of skitterish company,
That is all there is. Kettle boiling, pan frying,
the pages of another tepid novel,
        swimming through hands dog earing
the wilted petals flayed by the apathy of time.

ii.

I mark the time you are gone
Not by the notched hours
But by the inches of grass grown.
Where there is on some sun bitten days
Respite which proffers the opportunity—
To touch the blades with blades,
        and in removing their bodies
I can in some ways hammer the resounding
Clamour of your departure from memory,
Clawing you closer back to home.
And then, there are rain tortured weeks
Where the grass grows wild and tall.
During these meandering falls,
        it is through waterfall glass
That I can watch the land become
Bountiful—lunging towards clouds,
Clambering to cover your face.

iii.

The pond is denied resurrection,
This year—harvest of all hard seasons.
The caryatid flutes whistling the
The plasma of mountains to
            Its parched heart;
With what comes, thinly,
            through veins caked with the palm
Sugar-like sediment of the sloughed
hills, drowns the stale shorn skin of
Winter masks gathered by clumped reeds.

In time, there will be enough
            torn strips of jaws and cheeks
To reveal the muted stone faces
That have labored another birth.

iv.

That loneliness is momentary.
Until I have caught up with the noontime moon.
We, each, have been company for the other.
Comforting is the permanence
That kept company, also, my mother—
And when others have spread themselves far too
Thinly for pleasure outside of their homes:
I have hurdled the burdens of the homeland without
Another. A solitary task it is, to attend the
Daily wounds of the measured boundaries.
The umbilicals must be weeded else their
Offspring suffer—limbs must be culled from the elder pines,
            the tougher ones may again endure another year,
and in the absential void of composing in an
empty city of tins: I seek out the smallest hand of colour to
            relish.

v.

The stupid chair—with angles none can fathom.
A gift—a bloody gift, it was meant to be.
One measured length became six unmeasured cuts.
The butts of the long arms were uneven and rough.
The toes of the feet were duck angled and off—
        the stupid chair taunting every hammer
Blow with a resounding thud of permanence.
And on the third day—when its shoddy neck
        pushed the night sky to its heels—and teetering
The universe held its breath, ready to tumble—
I took the axe—and murdered the bloody chair,
With cathartic swings, spreading my arms like
The wings of a blood-lusting animal. Its splinters
became antennae in my flesh—and distantly the
Sing-song voice of the wood frame crackled to silence,
        and the sky fell gently on hair.

vi.

The hour is chaos. The day is chaos.
In absence of a woman's breast, instead, take refuge
In the breast of   the near wood; be
Gently clutched like a fatty meat slipping through its intricate
Intestines: after   so many bends
Trampling the bended discarded fingers, and toeing the vagrant
Eyes out of place   in the long faces
Of long trees—the body will be secreted from its anus:
An undigested   writhing fan of bone.
Curled the newborn—wailing among the long ferns, coddled
By roaming ticks, [They do not
Suckle the blood of visitors, less they are filth] will be tumbled at
The foot of an   injured bridge
Beyond a sign of fallen limbs crowned with a gospel that reads

    END.

vii.

The pregnant mollusk of mountain
Clasped shut—rising pries the stiff
Legs of hard skies—and coarsely
whines as it spreads wide; expels the
aromatic umbilical to life.

Secreted from its granite glands, rubs the
Tenuous braid of living, sighs
Tracing the filaments of peaks stretched
To the far fold until they all but disappear.

And slowly bristling the warbling
breath of July crushes over pine, until
The bending of them—all—in time, is
Akin to the drawn breath of an organ

come to terms with being in tune with

     agony.

viii.

Wild running river, soothe the sacred scarred shins
Violently rinsing the viscera of felonies rubbed
On all who journey here.
Violating redemption, renewal, stood erect
Under the soft christening phallus of feral light.
Soil does not cling—the chorum resonates,
The high note descends but does not bite.
All the sickness, fevered working, to maintain
the solemn toiling subsides. Do not move:
The pungent sex of new life watches, to
Suffocate all who break suddenly to hide.

ix.

The rhododendrons have turned to god
Bent their pallid stickly bodies down
for a hand of salvation.
Wavering on the brink of a pathetic demise
Forgiveness smothered them as a quilted
Continent of powdered haze.
The apathetic gloved hands to toil
Bag after bag upon the marinated throng—
Whose prickly tongues had all but riddled
The dry sun.
And now they thrive, thrive under
The tine of a brutal father whose eyes
Give no love and heart cares nothing for bloodlines.

x.

The austere American clavicle is a hill to die upon.
The agitated precipitous trail—summits—
From navel at the swamp-footed end of rural
Oblivion to the ledge overseer, whipping the
Braying trunks to pull, pull the mule-headed stubborn
Sun to bed; to bed in the murky harshness of euphoria.
And the rayless world coming to a crawling ORGASM
Sinks the yowling milky seed of a new night
Between the motionless thighs of damp skin.

xi.

The suckling pig's blood smells fine—
A sweet gritted paper filling
The senses of a nose in decline.
The coagulating patty of a fattened
          blood roux
Wafts like the copper serum of
A woman tipping her monthly communion
Down a porcelain gullet of
Fine white china at midnight, watching
Swirl and curl and tussle around,
Around, and around—turbulently
Dripping down the carnivorous sewer—
          gulping—gulping.
Pig's blood, man's blood, woman's blood,
Is all the same. Stark and tacky,
And given time, enough, it all dries to flakes
Of the same paper mud that blows
Away and leaves no trace of body.

xii.

By the flick, the quarter inch bares blade
And the brick brown chuck rattles at a break
Into the thick groin of brush at the root of
        twin trunks.
And the sex of the forest is dense and acidic
Enough—that to follow is a fool's errand
But there is no rush to be foolish—so
Bathed in the dust of ants and flies
Near the loose skin of moss and bark, I make
Bed and nap, until patience bears fruit.
One eye half open measures the one eye
Half closed, a bruised yellow blinking flower
Hidden between hostas and ferns—
And I, almost naked in the short pool of
Warm sunlight, run the foreign nose
Of pointed steel into the tip of domestic flesh.
Not enough to draw blood, but to remind
That blood must be drawn. And my other
Hand, as useless as a flaccid cock,
Limply tussles the grass in the whispers
        of celibate wind.
And the body in the brush shudders and it
Laughs, laughs and shudders—rattles
And laughs, happily not knowing,
That given time alone—it shall not live long.

...

The eye grows monstrous,
Vast and terrified.
Each threaded red canal
Gorges—rushing, the lahar;

        Rallies to trample the flung
        lush borders of far wild grass;

        Rallies to fear—abject and resounding
        panic, a dense and heavy breath

        conspires to collapse the red berries
        of meager lungs.

The eye fills the field of flowers
With flushed sorrow—the eye
Laden with the protracted yen

§

for living
Fills the field, so fills the eye
Seeking its ruin today.

In that second the breath,
The clasp, the clutch, the squeeze
Comes to halt a hare's scalp
From teeth of gritted steel:
Hanged, the round renews its
Mute slumber—and slipped,
The lean neck lowered to
Forage the wild grass.

...

The deceased cease to be deceased
      under the curdling sun.
Rigor limbs transpose to companion dust
      hand in hand with the palms
Of drifting flocks of pollen.
      Bones, dried, atrophy to earth meal
to which bushels of apples fall.
      Bruised and dying, first the skin
Peels to a dry crisp, then the sweet meat
      dries to leather, and in end the
Core—bared naked—sinks to the other realm,
      the shallows in the hides of grass.

xiii.

I have brutalised the forty foot pine

Rutting the rusted axe until sap wine ran the

Tongue of snarled neck— and baptised

The fine edged bush knife

Until it, too, rang dull.

For two hours and some minutes—was the cut,

And then it was culled. The collapsed limb

Was fed to the mouths of yearning thicket—

Soon, in winter, the carcass will

Reside in the crusts of snow—sculpture,

Of a summer death embalmed.

And after the field was scythed—

The pond's edge was drawn and quartered,

And imbrued, a confession was

Recorded from the last rites of a dying hog's hide—

a psalm of ash dusting its still feet.

After it all, there was nothing.

The cool evening breath sighed "be still"

And nursing burning calloused palms

I sat, and shared a beer with the plain

Sky. When drunk enough later, perhaps,

I shall conjure the courage to dance with her.

Tow my hands down the spine of her cupped back

to the snapping elastic waist. Lowering the skirt

And letting run my wild thirsts.

xiv.

Half-dozing, stirred to restlessness
As uninvited the north wind snaps
Through the unruly mass of lawn
Bending the congregation's eyes
of wilted necrotic tulips until they
Rise to sky—clutch back and forth,
Shuck families in leathered bands,
Ascend and shatter to a thousand
Pips of indigo swallows. Toes fan
with flushed red aroused flesh, cast
A net to the air—eyes bloom from poppy
Flecks to platters of sloe, and interred under
the tight throat is alive the chattering
Call to the coming clatter of the

lavished hunt.

xv.

The lolling tongue burdens
The placid chapped lips
Of a panting mouth—and comes
Writhing languidly to life when
Touched by the sweetened
Spit of sugar and river water.
Finger fed to seared cheeks,
Puffs and folds,
[the quorum of woods delicately awaits
            feeding]
As a weeping organ is put in place—
Seeps a moist breath—and gently
Paddling tattered feet slap whorls
Of mud into stale bog air.
Mutely, the revived limbs
Carry off cutting to the blown
Pane of settled water—leaving only
A crushing still, bar for the click
Of aged knuckles and the far off call
Of a black bear and her newborn
            young.

xvi.

Tangerine is the world,
And black is the pip.
Accosted by the bill of living,
Came rage—and came
                this recollection of a past
                life.
Why is the price
Of waking so steep, so high.
There are the skeletal remnants of
Those too poor to pay, or afraid
To run—left straggled on the scrambling
                climb.
What view exists from the summit?
When we reach the lip of that
                lauded orifice?
What view shall teary eyes land
Upon at the scalp of the world?

What view will be?

Shall it match the painting
                in the barn in the woods—
A tangerine world,
And black is the pip—
Or shall the world seem merely
                a gray flat skin,
And we the hairs upon its body.
The colour thriving in the
                threads unseen.
I can see those familiar hips
                swaying gently,
And without thought.
And when the eyes have glanced
                their fill.
Are we to descend as difficultly as we
Rose, or fall easily into that insurmountable
                abyss?

xvii.

The spruce are dying—strung with ill.
Sprung on them an elongated tensile death.
Malnourished limbs sorely bend—and run
Until the weight of hunger breaks their brittle
Will, the splinters flying—cast against the
Debris free sky, desecrating the hard paid still
And stills the chorus of beaks lapping
The refugees of turned soil.
And when all the spruce have perished—
The new saplings will be homed, and thrown
Over their soft fresh hair, will be the ash of bodies.

Exist within the disembodied state—
>   where to be, is to appear without [a monument lack a capitol]

Who
>   had hopes and dreams, and the usual wants, but to this life they are superflous.

It appears that what is to be done is to accept the discrete incarnations

>   the reawakening we as people don every morning

but no, discard this notion, beautiful Celine
We vomit, together, this stupefying repetition

>   purging in honour of the chronic being

the continuous strand of the addict—bingeing and offering. And though all around us
attempt suicide
>   and attempt to herd our sullied covers to the field that is grazed by fermenting
>   carcasses

We shuck them and this normality

Shuck our backs of brutality—and suck the sweet marrow of banality out of dawn

>   where through conscience married to the hours by breath and by the force of
>   attraction

We shall never be solitarily, or abandonedly alone.

"Look on my Works, ye Mighty, and despair!..."

But I am not mighty, nor shall I despair,
What works have I wrought from nothing—one
Life that tatters in the violent air.
What works have I, rushing with despair in the
Surging river from upstream somewhere,
built to stand aside the days. My home
Settles on thick poles of legs, whose feet sink
Into the quarrel of human wear. And a body
That is abducted, leaves only a scalp—kite—
On the neck of wind, and a salivating heart set
To the prongs of a broken sternum.
What love and friendship have I
Chiseled from the stone gut of so many
lands? I, who can count those who would cover
My body in cloth should I be bloody and torn—
Or those who without cause would call
and tongue the currents that slip between us—
On hands with many a severed finger.

"Look on my Works, ye Mighty, and despair!..."

How can one look—when the grit of childless
Rooms are glued to the eyes. I do not want such
Needles births, oh mothers, is there not a silence
Resoundingly clear enough for you. And if I did come to
Father the cut away limb that would grow
And foster that same pale fruit—eyes would not cry
Or mouth descry at their human nature.
What works, those who are mighty, do I hold.
See the field, I toil, see the desk, I hunch,
See the woman who has forgiven me all, and every
Morning arrived. Her body is the mightiest
Work I know. And no flesh of mine whittled
A single cut of that perfection. What works of
Yours compare to that ideal—what deed
transpires that could hurdle that ascent?
No work—no god—no world, can spew enough to
Cut low the coaxing face of that affection.

§

"Look on my Works, ye Mighty, and despair!..."

To look long and desperately and see only
empty girth. If in the void of night, and the void
Of day, and the void of countless filling moments
There solely sounds the roll of breath over body;
The body of foreign movements—articulation
Strangely abstract and the sudden snap of being
Lifted high and gone forever—then why
sully the shortest thing we are, with work—
"Look on my Works, ye Mighty, and despair!..."
What works are those? What works are those?
I look upon the wound bowels of your ego,
And see nothing but what has come before.
And why despair, mouthless voice, why despair—
I point to you, among the unsettled stars
And claim—you may be the king of kings,
But I am the man of all poor men. Driven by
Needs of flesh alone, I live, and shall die, to be

Forgotten.

The rain has come for hours—for hours the rain has run
To another place, down gutters, down streams, but now
The rain runs down the faces of glass, outside, to us;
Inside our gaze comes down upon the ruins of dead fish—
Lunging knives to pare the waists of brackish flesh—of
Soft flaked body, curled within the sack of softer hands.

> [& I imagine our waists broken in two by giant hands;
> nonchalantly and mindlessly handled—
> tossed into the snapping bath of oil—we are together]

The silence has come for hours—circling in shallows, its
Trajectory angled so that any given moment it is between us;
Mutely is conducted the rough plucking of leaves, the rallying
to eat, the offering of food, the uttering refusal (mouthed gently),
All theatre for the cinch of day; she cooks, slowly, and I watch,
chewing indifferently the tart butt of a summer plum, the tied knot
        of spiced skin.

> [& I imagine each bite to swim the riverine tongue,
> gulley of throat, canals of chest, to a hidden pond
> where it shall rest—a soothing balm to anguish]

The night has come for hours—slowly come on slipped like
Covers over thighs in the cage of shag and wood—
Night slipped to the loping gait of thick black hair tumbled
Down the mustard of her neck. Outside the night scents
Of damp and grass, moss, drowned bark, and the sodden
Throng of foliage. Inside the night scents of her—of
Unpacked things, tossed cloths, painted wood, of aniseed
And wine, and the briny viscous blood of olives.

> [& I imagine the elderly lines of groves spread
> far across the parched palm of field, the sun in
> flesh fingering the green buds she so loves]

The warmth has come for hours—hours the warmth floods;
Working separately, together: fold and press, hands of mine
To twist and cut—the legs and arms of her bend and clutch.
The sinew of calves, pulls and coils. The outside comes to sup
the warmth in humming mass, and to be hard and soldierly—

§

I bow to orders and lull the wings to still; I kill—and kill for her—
feast on the sorrow to snuff the soft haired bodies, still the
sheen of paper wings but for her, it is still—it is stilled.

[& I imagine the elderly lines of groves spread
far across the parched palm of field, the sun in
flesh fingering the green buds she so loves]

There are no doctors here
    To define this sky—so you must
        discard your perception of anatomy;
            do not frame the clouds as lungs
                huffing down upon the green and brown
                    buttes, but as eyes—that nonchalantly covet
                        the grounded nature of our minuscule feet

and the breadth not as a chest but as breasts
    from which intermittently seeps a loose milk
        and the lines of mercurial lightning not as tongues,
            but varicose veins, a mar upon the perfect calves of sublime legs.
                Follow the flesh with your eyes, and rise, crooking the neck. See,
                    there's a forbidden thing there, above, it the hymen of a vestal web;

Sacred thing that is yet to be pressed
    by our lacerating affection. There are no
        doctors here, and none of our company made
            strides to such a lofty racket—we can then, instead,
                only let loose to blow in the wind rags of words slapped
                    together—harshly, and quickly—to frame this fleeting juncture.

Woman of the blue eyes—who mutters of horses and the hips of mountains,

      sanitises her child—the world at her feet; floating above the mire

yearning for the world without filth—her daughter born into the

Paddock of composting fruit skins, skin shining, clean—yearning for

      the things of mother's past. Youth sloughing the filth that will stick in time.

And why not whimsy,   in place of sacrifice?

      Sensitivity to the stirrings of inner shamans—who slap the river stones

And cull the entrails of lost children, conjuring the bean that flourishes.

      Orchid of children, they bloom so young, and wander a lifetime wilting.

And why not whimsy,   in place of sacrifice?

We could not scribe a greater comedy than the life of persons on continents,

So many afflicted by the disease of looking up to the lives of angels who never land.

Black

Born lousy—

dropped from the hot clouds, a head first valkyire,

whose breath—wet mist—respired on marsh fat.

To hit, every razor lipped branch on the way down.

And each was a year,

       by thirty the flayed comedy of the frail bones was in full swing.

A third act,

    long gone,

          a fourth come and whore-like devoured,

               a fifth, six, seventh…all gone.

Consumption became a real life skill.

A degree earned in pirouetting though

          plate glass windows of others' homes.

If only I had ever married my first love at eight.

Kimberly-Fernandez, Latina

                    Dream with a slip of earthen skin—

under the remission addled

pohutakawa

I tried to grasp her hand.

Grappling with the pang of adolescence—

§

how the birds laughed—she, curtsying away, tongue tip dancing

along the enchantments of isolation.

Adolation never pays son—dream father whispered,

and now you're tar stuck and feathered.

Cape of the dead birds—christened the lonely vessel of my mountain mind.

And every bird that's flown since,

has been another stripe down the tiger skin of my back,

another tooth in the maw.

The taste for flesh never ebbs—

is what I wished they had taught—

and now, the taste of flesh is all I can stomach.

Red

Laudanum, please—

a drop or two as the viscous holy water for the eyes:

for the suffrage of her eyes—

wet the crackling cellophane of aged sclera,

and wiped, we witness the vibrant oils of her unearthed irises.

That suffrage, the one last vote not slipped into the mouth of the ballot.

Pale cheeks and the etched folds of years lent to the rebar facade,

her spangled iron work face—

never had one juried such stoic flesh.

The years privy to the declination of her husband,

and yet, she prolonged.

§

Vows, her recitations of faith—never beyond the prairie edge she ventured,

incarceration was then voluntary—

faithful, untested, the flesh sullied by voyaging no further south

than the northern plain.

And on the day she opened her suffering to our ears

and in shame let on that death had finally come for her—

was skirting her grey hair—

tears fell, and all was quiet. What to say—

when the endless cliff erodes and is lost to the undisturbed water?

Gold

Two thirty seven am—

Head surgeon supped coffee and wound the umbilical

Round and round the throat of the boy,

Ejected four pounds eight ounces:

he was a hanged man as he fell from the sacrificial uterus of his mother,

tearing along the asymptote of her groin,

lurching at the end of the tether.

                                 [the whole bloody room
was at the end of the tether]

One world to another—one celestial egg to the grand sandbox

of Boston Children's delivery floor.

        Have you ever seen a hanged man dance?

     §

Not ever.

      In the civilized today of death

by quiet words slipped to prisoners flat packed

and shot with a prick that only a flea could see.

No suffocation tango—just a stillness whilst inside the

whatever is rendered to fatty waste.

One minute later—they unwrapped the trachea—by turning the body counter clockwise,

          and then clockwise, and giving it a hard shudder.

Breached, they had spun him like a gyroscope—

trying to find the center of the universe.

He did not cry—the brown gold viscera of his mother remained—

the coming, leaving gold scars

      to run down the thighs of her nights alone.

It strides   with spring rain—
Stumbles with first winter   snow.
      Between the snow   and next rain
There is a   dismembered   absence.
      Between the spring rain   and first snow
There endures   everything.
Where the most damning   rule   in those

Gelid months—

> *when the faces are shunned*
> *the lick of sun and the warmth of*
> *salt crusted skin, humid breath is bartered*
> *for the thaw of charred husks—*

Is the burial of bodies under the constrictor
       of cloth.

Every specimen   scratching,   jotting
Unknowingly upon a calendar
       of constrained passerby.
The solstice becomes penned not by
The length   of day, but by the length
                       of thigh.

Pale legs assembled as sundials,

Casting backwards to the amputation of
each cramping film. Where between
the first snow and spring rain—
underneath the matted peel
is revealed a tender
and unsullied
art.

A marriage has ruptured.

Are they all not such tenuously lived things: contracted love.

Can one contract attraction. Is it a malaise—

and if so, is there a cure?

Could such hard labour have ever been thought to be so delicate.

Promises unto death. But death, falsely, is thought to come at the end—

when really, death can be there from the birth.

Death can live in us everyday, and rise in the morning with us,

savour a hot black coffee, and appreciate the mysticism of a sunrise—with us.

Ruptured, I have fulfilled my promise early; to part when death has come,

which is now, and before, and after.

Fragility bears poorly under tension, and so, it was rendered—

vividly and suddenly, the collapse.

It is coming to fall now. In winter—it is too cool, and summer—too brazen.

There are four seasons—but only one worth living.

Spring perhaps when reticent, is glorious—

when the young learn that to be loud is to invite attention.

Fall, when the leaves turn their backs on the world, curl, and die so elegantly:

that is the time worth being.

And so their going is foretold—cumulating in a voluntary mass suicide that we relish.

There are those who refuse and stubbornly live through the winter,

but they are the limbs of nature not worthy of respect.

See, however, that it is never sudden, and yet still so stark.

Contrarily I conferred change in an instant, poorly and without care,

adoration, or affection.

This cyclic death, it comes every year and yet we never part from the seasons.

§

We endure, and bear, and treasure, and come time and again—

we return. Yet, with connection, we surrender.

We give nothing, and take all. Churches within ourselves.

Pastors of the flock. Shepherds of barren hills. We peer to the coast,

see the clouds sending their children to the sea and assume

it is our hand which turns the hours, and days.

No, it is not. It is not this hand, nor that mouth, nor that breast, nor that leg.

No human flesh has taken part in life.

No human flesh has prodded me to be so abjectly wanton.

     A marriage has ruptured.

     And when ruptured, the jellied flesh of its history was served for all.

     I was not ashamed for them to see my secrets.

     My secrets are merely reminders of their own.

All the woman offered was twenty dollars;
two dirtied tens printed on tarnished and muddied paper
for the black shelf gathering ash in the garage—
I did not bother to say, nor did she know to ask,
if once a newborn had languished upon the third shelf.

Shelves carry secrets, and live longer than us;
so I have figured, that sometimes, the worst of us
is found long after we have abandoned the furniture of our world.
Remaining silent—I contemplated whether
the vivid reminiscence of that decaying child

would make what was plainly a poorly kept memento
ascend in value: worth more in her eyes, knowing eyes
had once shut forever upon it. Truth being, we pay dearly
for the voyeurism of such things—and so inevitably
I expose the past, always, and so follows an extruded

reliving of that pain. It is the opening of a door to a room
in which lives a thing that really is no longer living—
Rendered alive enough only as a reminder that it is parting.
I have done what all children do: gently dismembered living
things as a sign that I love them more than anything.
Drawn petals from the stem, and words from unmoving mouths.

I have done—that—which all infants do: caused pain
only to see if pain is worth causing.
I have done what all children do: lie boldly to my mother
so that I would not lose what tenuous love remained.
On sodden days I have buried uneaten lunches in the loose

earth of the garden, and hidden open eyes
under the dark expanse of covers.
I have done what all children do: wither in a cool place,
where it is quiet, and no ears can attune to my soft crying.
I whispered vengeance into the gentle winds that carry

through all the homes of the lonely young.
Is it that inconceivable? That one can die but keep living.
It is a black shelf of daily mortality. I dreamt of a buried placenta.
Buried beneath the black shelf. The ground weeping a coagulated
gruel between my toes, and on the bottom was set a stained blanket.

§

Stained with patches of what gathered on the damp floor.
Marker to a childhood rubbed in the soft cotton of neglect.
No one ever acquires the shelf.
They gladly carry away the deep teal cat hair clotted lounger;
> the mottled and faded Moroccan rug with the ripped stitching—that really was made in Turkey;
> the chipped and ring stained teak table—proudly made by Danes but less proudly kept;
> the gilded ash pots;
> hand built frames;
> the warped glass;
> the battered brass tray.

There is a caravan of keepers who take it all but the black shelf—sitting remotely.
A void lingers at its feet, and I am saddened as its isolation.
No one ever carries away the shelf.
> They cannot keep or appraise the malaise of that piece, and so it gathers ash—the flotsam of desertion—and quietly stands whispering upon the wall.

Such difficulties in the placement of words to a lip;
restlessness to a hip;
venturing to skin;
a monumental clasp it is—to twine tongue to a tongue:
Is that the conjoining of flesh to flesh,

> some muddying of boundaries physical and spiritual
> so enticing that one fears its loss so much
> as to never transpire to attempt at all?
> I am consumed to think of the sculpting of lovers.
> Often have I studied the thousand portraits of them one morning—

only to return to study the next night, and again.
Countless times I have watched the plays,
consumed the prose,
regurgitated the prayers of what lovers are to us.
What crowns those who are deemed to have loved—

> and culls the peasantry of those who have not?
> I have thought love similar to tilling a field.
> Some years are spent turning the soil,
> turning the laughter, turning the tears,
> turning the intimate nights—where one previews

the taste of those places—open.
And it is hard; hands are never free of cuts, and welts, and blood;
one's fingers are used to search that hard ground,
and denominate which flesh is to be sacrificed to conjure fertility.
And some years conclude in nothing,

> nothing but a field of soaked earth; rows opened but barren.
> The terminus is found, and it is hollow;
> the repercussions of the infertile end
> is what makes the vacant paddy resplendently callous.
> One is broken here—or lives in a suffering defeat,

abdicating their humanity.
This is the cultivation of the lover, the convulsion of living,
the compulsion of the honest want.
The sodom of the vine stems from this.
It is why we thrive in planting the crop,
so much more controllable than what lives in us.

§

It is why we till, why we grow, why we reap,
why we take and mar, constrict and asphyxiate,
repeated, and repeated, pressed until the essence of it
runs between our toes.
If not the warmth of another, then the warmth of crushing

something between the wants that drive us.
Yes—this is why the vine becomes the obsession
of the lover who has not loved:
it holds closest to what is perceived to be felt
when the coursing blood of another is within your maw.

To assume adulthood, is not to presume the donning of responsibility—
but to embrace those evils to which we voluntarily consign ourselves.

I have elected my failings:

as to Drink, and to Fuck, and to Write—perhaps, occasionally
I will Draw but my Drawings are always relegated to encompassing
the recollections of my vastitude. I am not ego, nor hubris—
I am neither humble, nor servile:
I am the expanse, and I am the many, and the few.
I am to always wake in the skins of others.
At places of work, I worship those who I have become.
In places of lust, and homeliness, and engendered vulnerability—
I become incarnations of those whom I covet.
Proclamations of mastery over the rote nature of days is,
perhaps, the least meaningful of ways in which to spend the spoiling hours
and brittle seconds that are unreclaimable.
Be honest in that we face the incalculable perdition of biology,
the clocks ever ticking, ever chiming, ever grinding until the day
they are submersed in stillness.

And of Drinking,
I have elicited that scotch has become the sole body worth imbibing.
For a good drink must burn, it must mar, and that wound must be physical,
conscripted from reality:
fashioned from palpable sensations—
newsworthy emotions that buckle ones veins and turns liver to goose flesh
flayed in some way that has rendered its worth to matters of texture and chemistry.

And of Fucking,
it is concrete that the act is pure secretion of instinct
in the most vulnerable point of imposition:
that gateway within a gateway—and to fuck is never for pleasure
but to be for one minute a God, and to own time as one would own a fly;
where the impulse to discard that moment to nothing is power.

And of Writing,
conclusions have been drawn that no other greater waste of human cognition exists.
Words ejaculated from the scratchings of discursive thoughts—
ladled with the burden of being mortal and fleshly,
and yet only the eager could unravel their spirit.
Writing is to refuse water to those dying of exposure,
and printing words is to fountain wine to the faithful.

§

And of Writing—
I say nothing more—but that it is the parturition of paper and ink,
and when flung in the scoffing faces of the literate is the truest instance of courage.

And of my Drawings,
they are a poor representation of a girth of emptiness;
only ever incarnations of woman, man, or the both—
together, entwined.
To draw for the self, is to copulate with the inner workings of want.
As of my drawings—
they are the ground upon which I worship—
their bodies are the bodies upon which I lie.
Where one grasps a vision of legs splayed,
the spatchcocked buttocks of a sleeping woman showing her doorway
opened to the cool night, the most visceral cove of flesh scratched before you—
red faced,
I see only the embrace of honest nature:

The lines of paradise in the folded veil of her womb.

I came into my own as a reviled man.

Anxiety is the constrictor.

It coils in my arms.

The hosepipe vein to my heart is its body.

I have put my hands to her throat.

Clasped the pulse from her trachea.

I could have so easily crushed the wind from the sky in her gaping mouth.

Pried the lolling tongue from between the pearl teeth in the void—

have elicited the cavity of her chest to have sung—

singularly, I conquerer, could have conquered—

tossing aside her body into the tide of the night.

Bodies have become unseen in a black ocean.

Why not again?

How would they find us, both?

Sinking into the triangular remiss of the black sea.

Swallowed once more into the gash of her womb.

Sinking into the foaming agitation.

I have held her to the moon.

Have held her legs unto the stars—

howled the name of her.

Many of my friends have died.

One was separated into two.

He was once a man, and then was two—

one without a manhood, and one without a heart.

How easily could we join the dead?

Too easily. So mortal, so fragile, could we shatter and reform.

§

I have seen the bone rent from a grey child.

I thought the child deceased—and was proven correct.

And I have seen the red flesh of her mouth of mouths.

I have put my hands to her throat.

They made a puppet of the reviled corpse of that child,

and made her dance along the dirty street

in the unloving way a toy moves when plied by the gripping hands of immaturity.

And how she jived, adolescent shoes rapping,

little dead thing that hopped to the four count fix.

And I come back into my own.

And once more I gazed the snake wind through the marrow of my extremities.

And again I murder.

And again we collect the rigor'd kid.

And again we swim in the ocean.

It is cold, and tastes of salt—brackish fingers down our throats—

and we regurgitate not one but two unmoving eyes.

This is my night. This I dreamed for days. For weeks. For years.

The slumber was wretched.

I sought women who sought to be used.

I sought women who sought to use me. I

saw a rotting child corpse in the cupboard of my room.

I saw the dead woman swimming towards the stars.

I attempted to drown my mind in the beach at the lions head.

And woke—with the snake coiled around my groin.

And in that house, I was the serpent within the sheets.

The suicide was committed on a Tuesday in November.
It was raining, clearly, from the thousand small lakes
that had formed in the thousand minute holes in the road.
The deceased had stood in the rain without an umbrella—
had been observed as being still under the deluge.
It is considered normal—not wanting to get wet.
And so, on a Tuesday, an abnormality was marked.
One citizen, without care and lacking attention to the self,
was seen to be prone in the storm as others hurried,
others sped, from one point in the town to another.
And it was also seen that this blip in existence was smiling.
It wore the smile of someone at peace,
enamoured with the the enfolding world.
One witness is said to have detailed how delicately
the water beaded over and down the ridges of the deceased's cheekbones.
How the water fell like waterfalls from the contours of their face.
On this Tuesday, in November, the town was in full swing.
You see, a Tuesday is the most frantic day of our conformed week.
It is the day after the lull, and the day before the crest.
It is the day of bills, and actions, and meetings.
It is the day for loneliness and the magnification of loss.
Tuesdays are the most laboriously obtuse of days.
Abstract and nebulous.
It is a day made for only the most strenuously attuned.
But on most Tuesdays, a person will survive.
They will collapse at the finish line, and contend with crushing inwards,
until compressed into a singular ball of anguish.
And so, Tuesdays have come to be known as the origin of want.
We, from a collective gasp of anguish, erected happiness (and solitude)
from the withering relentlessness of this day.
Against these rules, the suicide was committed on a Tuesday in November.
It is said that the body was dissected.
That any who had seen the suicide would be traumatized,
but no witnesses came forward: no one had seen—only, all had felt.
A community can feel when one is gone.
When the abnormality is excised.
With any removal of the body, there is left a hole.
After the act, the street was returned and repaired.
Not a trace lingered of the body that was pressed into the asphalt.

The suicide was committed on a Tuesday, in November.
It was raining, clearly, from the thousand and one small lakes
that had formed in the thousand and one minute holes in the road.

It was there.
The letter that was forced into the fissure
between today's junk circulations and yesterday's forgotten coupons;
often, almost assuredly, the news of something mundane
that had been unshackled.
The yellow carcass was crumpled.
The corner was bent and folded upon itself.
Vagrant origami had imposed pressure until, like anything,
it took the form of its oppressor.
Yellow indicated culture.
Only lovers of letters used yellow vassals.
The minutiae of rote boredom
was routinely sent in white:
sacrosanct in unblemished purity.
Yellow was dirty—
the message was more alive below yellow slips.
Unravelling a colored envelope
was like undressing the legs of a hot pickup—
it always went somewhere good, and if not good,
then at least a get-off. There was a stain on the underside.
Coffee. Artifact of a morning struggle.
Lipstick was present where it had been fixed.
Ripples of lip flesh could be carefully discerned.
I was always seduced by the myriad intense details of a mouth print.
Pressing my own lips to the print on the letter surfaced
the awareness of stealing an intimacy from the sender.
I dreaded the accosting of my minutes—
of which I had far too few—
by the clutter that inevitably tumbled from the neat packages
that all clutter is announced in,
but this wasn't neat: it was messy.

Mythology is set into the daily life in ways one rarely reckons.
A letter—appearing as incarnation
of a wish granter's accommodation, is common myth.
Rubbing is parlayed for tearing.
A tongue's run across the bitter adhesive,
like a lover of gold's fingers running across an elemental brocade.
This action can be both erotic and medicinal,
yet the process is by far the most rewarding of the ceremony.
The content in the mass produced gifts of nothing
is pressed from wisps of composted thoughts.
Days once existed where a letter brought on its bow,
always,

§

a show of something important—
but now there is an inundation of letters,
and all they bring is the smell of shit and pseudo-urgency.
They appear dressed like the letters of history but no longer are they letters.
The most common allusion is that a letter was always something sent,
that could be read and regarded [disregarded] before being disposed of.
Letters, however, have always truly been concocted of people.
The human want—the message:
a body which conceals either passion or suffering.
Especially when stuffed with the tender filling
that accompanies such human failings.

In my life, I am [was] beset by letters.
Commonly…though less now,
they come [came] to me as women.
I went to them avidly. In this I am assured.
Younger days were less confused.
I took them for what they were.
Moments that would pass.
Now, however, I grip each woman that offers
the rarity of her compassion to me with an addict's clutch.
The male has known for centuries
what now is not merely sanctioned for the few.
That woman is the perfect letter.
She can contain, at once, all and nothing.
She can withhold and, at once, quickly erupt in spurious hostility—
and then, in seconds, descend with palmfuls of seducing tranquility;
in one bar whispering what is needed—
in another uttering the thing that unravels a body
like yarn unravels from a ball.
It is realistic, then, that at our core there is nothing but a hollow chamber.
I have known this for decades. In this I am obsessed.
All the letters I have received,
I have stuffed viciously into my gut [perhaps this has contributed to my growing belly]
but it is not enough. And now that I am no longer receiving as many—
I no more have much
with which to occupy the vacancy of my mislaid organs.

There are not many coming.

Those that come are precious.

The days are long between the red flag falling.

Today, a yellow letter arrived.

I will read it twice, and keep it on my desk.

It will live for years before it, too, is swallowed by my famine.

The house was rural, and quiet.

Thick forest abutted the long lawn on the East corner—

a slope of grassland slipped away to the West

towards a blinking eyelash of stone-littered shore

arced elegantly around a whisper of land that lead North.

In fall and early winter the sea fog was gently encouraged

to teethe its way up the hill to the South windows of the bedroom—

and so, when first opening your eyes,

you were welcomed by the face of a cool vaporous river

writhing on the storm-glass: jowls pulled by the friction of the warm home,

scalp pushed onwards by the hands of the frigid sea.

And once the fog had passed

you could run your hands over the smooth extremities

of the floor to ceiling windows

and gather the coarse dusting of salt

that had stowed in the gut of the vagrant cauliflower bodied brume.

Thickly wooded and mute—

the forested boundary was sulkily ambivalent

to all happenings on the land.

A relapsing cancer sloughed the hair from its body

until only the anemic skeletons of its many trees remained.

In spring, it ebbed to remission

and the head of thick brush reappeared.

Songs carried from near that place: odes and wailings.

I tell no one that on some evenings I was distinctly aware

of a spirited young woman yowling towards the kitchen openings.

§

And once, I saw her dash from the broken tree line

towards our door; tumbling in a manner that was hauntingly expired.

And as I rushed to close the entrance to our home

she wasted to projections of impeded dusk,

above her appearing a flock of geese hocking insults on their way to warmer grounds.

Come spring and into summer the sun would disperse the frost.

The ground would dew.

Brooks would once again flourish.

The first young of the land would have fresh footfall

upon the seeded and birthing earth.

Soil would turn under the strain of myriad limbs.

Chattering voices would be heard in the early sunrise—

a community convalescent in the waking minutes. In later hours—

stars would become distinct in a distant bloom of light

thrown rug-like over the cusp of land and expanding sky,

and one could open the sills to the night.

I lived a lonely year in that house,

rural—and quiet. And always—a clock would keep its time.

This clock, a large clock, was on the largest wall—

accompanied by nothing else.

The inside of this home was spartan but loved;

the outside was wild, and loved even more.

Night decided that we should walk the grounds—
was more to why we were walking
but stalking intuition was a failing ever puncturing
lungs with which sapped the breath of life &
spring, two weeks past, receded
and so, the night still gently lit was laced with cool breeze that
would flit home well before nine.
It seemed the perfect scene to indulge exploring
history within the folds of antiquity.
Clear, now still, the viscerally crumpled cotton
Deeply wound around the porcelain body—at odds with
ombre of tan and brown,

the green thrush of brush below dark oceanic sky—
and the sanguine flecks of gem freckled neck which fell
as if dabbed with the tip of bristling hair upon the world.
The neck funneling a current of all which came and went,
when walking one could not help but frequently gaze back—
anchored to this singularity of flesh.
At that time, even once the sun had set,
there was light to see without the need for lamps,
lending an unending air to the day—
where one could feasibly apply such disbelief
as to think the sun had never truly set at all.
That really it had merely dimmed from exhaustion—

and lay slumped over the slight crest of the world.
This twilight affect overcame all but one secluded lawn,
Where a true still darkness would preside.
The clearing would transform to a bear's den of black
that would subsume a body, dissolving its facets
until there was no part of it distinguishable from the unlit canvas
that was the forest, sky, and earth.
When one raised their eyes skywards
here it was another sky that greeted them;
a small aperture of clearing exposed multitudinous stars
that seemed to overwhelm and calm simultaneously.
Infinite pin pricks of distant light, clustered, overlapping, jostling,

all competing to be seen and placed within this realm of visibility.
Not one star could be ignored,
yet it was the scarlet in the dark that consumed,
and how one could forget the endless night above,

§

and around the cloth, that rustled imperceptibly,
came other sounds emanating from an entire unseeable world.
One could assume that, perhaps, it was the nature of us all
to perceive beauty with un-level eyes and expectations; flaw within us all—
to be drawn to what seems infinitesimally unimportant,
placing it far upon the pedestal of wants and desires.
But there was this body more dense than the arrayed stars,
which are presumed to be the heaviest parts of existence.

And still, tonight,
to think of the blushing in the night,
the deep imposing silence,
the quiet of being separately together on the stage of grassy field;
North of the pine bodied shrine, and South of the slate roofed houses—
none which could be seen; being separately together in the darkness,
where sound was the indicator of life,
and so the thousands of stars above came to us as the muted dead,
With only the supping of breaths in the shadows mattering at all.

The rain came on slowly.
A "small rain" as it would be said here.
To my eyes it was not slow—but merely a gathering rain,
draped film upon film, braid among braid, bead atop bead.
The fog-laden tide of the river mystified the distance—
and set all in a frame of suspension.
Tall treelined banks rubbed the sky
until it, indistinguishable, became the grey river neck.
When divorced, the river was enough to overwhelm
but together with the land
it became magnified in its rarified ability to amplify
the desolation that was home in the mountains.
The long hem of the coursing surge was known,
but today became unknown.
Stone bridges that bound invisible territorial scars were no longer familiar.
Brotherly brickwork could not recognised;
patterns of mottles and age-worn groups of stolen masonry
were suddenly constellations I had not ever recalled.
Singularly terrifying was the realisation
that I was again a stranger to the water,
but added to that was that I could no longer remember the names of the streets,
the smooth days-worn granite boulders,
or the gangly leaning pines.
A melancholy was present
as we wound alongside the thin slit path gently carved between the air and water.
As if to comfort the enveloping dolor, we aptly spoke of sadness and beauty—
experimenters on what love was to the selfish and love to the selfless.
If, perhaps, cerulean or azure had been an organ of the palette
that painted the surrounding backdrop,
or even the daubed auburn of fall—
we would have likely remained silent
and merely stared at the isolating seduction of it all.
Rarely did that which we felt ever come from the gathering air—
but rather it came from the seasoned winds of a place far away:
the skin of someone not from here.
It all was and is a litmus to the numbing insinuations
that the loneliness grouped within me has bred.
And, so, we spoke—shadowed by the voice
of an overwhelmingly morose sob that would echo and rap the steep shore banks,
knocking against our dulled sensibilities;
we adult creatures, adult beings, adult things—
agitators, churners, and bringers of such a passive lust to the normalcy of it all…

The river came on slowly, and the small rain gathered quietly at its shins.

Covenant

Do not the bear the covenant lightly—

Nor open doors to the tangerine locust

Hordes strung upon the bowed horizon.

With haste they come over the fields of wheat—

harvesters harbouring a devouring slave-hunger:

Haltingly the hand-softened sky repeals its anguished

skin to them—as they race across the

Soft hairless buttocks above its thighs.

The galloping wild—cavorting in their ways; tumbling,

Unseemly is the populace outside the walls of the spiritual.

And within, they pray and cower, and pray, stymying their

Soft shelled bodies beauty beneath nets of night cloth.

On the lapels of the virgin barbs is hooked the essence,

The hairy chested heaving thought—that no prayer

Can subdue nor send to the reaches of the human canvas.

Do not bear the covenant lightly—for to love a servant

Of the celibate compass—is an unrequited sacrifice.

To open doors to the lungs that are closed to

To any breath but that upon the morning crow—

A flesh never touched is a flesh worth hunting.

I shall open my door to the lungs that are closed:

We shall see how long devotion can hold its breath.

Could a colour be fall;   an iris be seasons;

Do we tire of the lack of choice?

How I tire, of the few from which we can choose to swaddle the world.

      Where have all the other colours gone?

         To which other land have all the colours dissolved?

A young student once argued,
                  that what is corporeal is never what truly endures.
What bullshit.
          What is corporeal is all that endures:
The Gods of women and men are untouchable,

intangible,

       and so never exist.

The mouth bites down into the citrus body of an orange,
and runs the bright sweet iridescence of its death towards the lungs.
And runs its riverine entrails into the breath,
becoming sweetly vivid—passing to the air.

Could fall be a colour;
         the colour of skin in the pale luminescent morning still—

where there is pollen nestled upon the thousand antlers of hair.

And my hand upon the infinite parts of that body.

To breathe pollen from the skin—
          is sustenance.

To breathe the vastitude from the feminine—
          is existence.

A colour can be put to paper,

or cloth, or bread,

or bared skin—

Truth is that a scarlet is one true meter of our constant internal violence.

To ingest the second hand breath from a strangers lungs—
is the sharp excising of the gratuitous fat of life.
To respire profoundly the used air from a used throat, is to breath the very body of
    another.
Could a colour be fall? Could a colour become the tangerine sting of cold upon a
    warmly wrapped breast.

Form—dressed in leaves, that never lulled to a wilt.

That is how I know her.

I know she is the forest that lived through winter.

Once, there was attempted an urge to pry the leaves covering her breasts

    apart,

        to deem whether her skin was bark.

The leaves refusing to part

    had snapped away the hand,

        and wavered in a way that was reminiscent of an impending eclipse.

Her forest would rustle as she approached.

        And would whisper as she loudly departed—

voice singing of the coming of fall

        from around the unseen way of tomorrow's day—where

some tomorrows the leaves would glisten from the rain.

        Drops would be hanged slowly from her extremities,

            kicking then stilling,

to eventually land on the ground with a barely audible step.

    Once,

        I had been fast enough to snatch a recently cadavered drop from the air,

            and let it slip onto my tongue.

                The water was cold, fresh, and slightly sweet.

There was no hint of earthiness.

        The soil dared to only watch.

This was her water—her purity.

I do not conceive of days waking to the forest having withered.

        There are times when it grows frail, but always to return.

Though, of late,

§

there are leaves scattered at the altar of the bed.

They have dried and cracked—buried in the soft shag of rug.

Exhumed—

I do not tell of these fallen specimens.

They are interred in the wood drawer of the bedside:

bound to the sealed air.

Our tomorrow is delicately slipping to past light.

I know there will be a day when she is bare,

And her skin will still glisten when barren.

Hard Light leaks from behind the ear.
Hard Light behaves as if it is a clear fluid—
somewhere between water and a molasses in its viscosity.
You can bear it in your hands, but only for a moment, and then
it will run through your fingers as minutes through the days. Perhaps,
approaching the asymptote—the years of our declination, a select
few memories will have pooled and gathered for a final
savouring. It has about it a musical quality similar
to an East wind, where from nothing it comes
whistling, and with ease sloughs away the
solemnity of today. The allure
of Hard Light, you see,
considering its
ephemeral
nature,
is how it
matures and
recedes like the maple
leaf. The corners of our tiny flat,
and soon our slightly larger home,
and perhaps in years our greater family
—will curl with it, opening their bellies collectively.
It is, as I have uttered before, present during the day as
well as night. In so many solitary gatherings have I spent hours—spying
upon the Hard Light from behind discarded bodies. At times, the appearance
of it mimics the outlines of a woman—with a peculiar, and familiar gait.
I am sure, it has collected the slight mannerism of those other
hands through which it has swum. Hard Light, being

independent, can never be curtailed
or committed—but if loved willingly enough,
will remain faithfully until the day it evanesces abruptly.
There is no point in calculating such a date. And soon, with
the coming snows, I will construct a room to be kept especially apart;
and when guests shall come to dine, I will escape, and from there perceive
them all—submersed—within the oddly provocative alacrity of its presence.

The body is flung. It comes alive as a thousand paper sheets,
fluttering on the whistling rails of breath.
      It becomes flotsam on the parades in the quiet lunchtime hour.
The shine of fresh nails pursues the decomposing banks of paper;
      what is it that they sought? Words? Of which there are plenty.
Mound upon mound of paper, there are hundreds stained,
      hundreds warped, hundreds untended, all the disemboweled
drawers disgorging entrails full of words.
      Some are scarred with complex words, some simple,
many with words wrought of words, some with words wound from non words:
      what is it, that they sought? And how they looked,
the free flying wreaths of essays, and those schemes, and illiterate plans—
      swiftly constructing rattan constellations in the peach autumn sky.
When the hip of the world sat on the right, they swept to the left;
      and as the hip sunk to the left, they swayed right,
circling the thighs of the land. And if I was to snatch the paper from the air,
      and stack it face upon face, and choose the stained for the heart,
and pure for the body, and torn for the hands, and worn for the face:
      I could engineer the compound curves and static intricacy of a naked form.
A nest for what squatted openly in the gutter.
      And when the hours attuned to fatigue and began to wind into a silence,
one could peer into the body I have built, pulling from its resisting flesh
      a single sheet. From where they pulled they would have in their
hands the story of a collective entity.

      Tonight, I have tugged a folded square from the damp of its mouth;
when opened there sprouts a pistil of words at its core,
      lain lazily under a refractive saliva:

      "I am imperfect. I am poorly bonded. See how my body withers.
        I am the cacophony of your loss."

Gaol was a courtyard within a triangle of three steps.

She was a streetwalker who I knew as Maria.

What a beautiful name.

Her purse was always full of vacant mens numbers.

She fed me once when I was hungry.

During the rain, I sheltered her

under a spirit shattered black umbrella

That I could only afford because it was thrown away.

The fabric was velvet. The frame was bent;

A stray rib pierced at a quarter to five.

  I recorded the wet leaves that orbited her

  as she stood on the corner block.

  A forest beauty incarcerated in that place—

  a place without a single tree.

  I once took pictures of her naked—

  I was ashamed, but never threw them away.

  A Goddess in every right—black boots

  worn at the toe—fitted blue denim jeans, and the cut leather

  80s ripcord jacket that let slip just enough.

  She was a savant within.

    Choreographer of the dance of street politics.

    The words she found could have bloodied the town.

    Maria was a religious name.

    If I saw her on a cross, I'd not look away.

    That night—they'd gone too ripe on the new

    prime minister.

§

I think Maria would have made a grand minister.

Good with cash. Good with a stick.

Knew when to work it—but really,

she's playing a game with the chords of your loins.

There isn't a single care there.

Maria. I hear her confess in the third act of my dreams.

The rosary of her tongue wraps around the trachea.

Maria—immaculate mother of the streets.

Candle of Arctic sun

      burnt incessantly for over half of a year.

Having bathed within the peninsula

      of her back.
Crescent of her low arch,

          a pool of clarity—rippled with limbs—

is cool and still:

within which nude portraits dive.

            Many arms through the stream of her spine,

Conduct life upon the calcified strata of her bone,

In the half-light,

have wrapped twine from her neck

                    around
                    the mounds
                    of parched
                    throat:
hidden dates beneath her breasts.

          A brusque air sweeps over the sagging husks of chest.

It has become frigid—fiercely biting;

                numbing, yet short of harsh.

      Tenderly ambient: awakening

     stirs the hairs staggering to the clutch of groins.

            In the peninsula of her spine—choirs have sung

And longed, in voice, for the stars rising

              to never fall

         [and yet, their entrails twist down, eternally].

There is nothing here—

         in the pout of our lands.

An imprint of her buttocks in the snow.

A press of her warm flesh into the stiff air.

Saliva condensed to white mounds above the ice hard ground—

§

Who wields—to draw the first [and last] woman upon the sky.

Warmth of body melting her symbol into the land.

Arctic sun shows its hand. Cupped among the lucent grove:

The Arctic sun has resolved and all have settled to the dark of her coast.

In the peninsula of her back: cities drown.

HOYA—Ascending.
Delicately watered every morning.
     First skin grazed by morning light.
Taking care to spread the rainfall gently about its waist.
     Drifts water along the long fall of its neck.
HOYA: weeping and celebratory in stature.
          Gaze stapled to her.
       Watching her turned on the lathe of want.
    Long arms drawn from fragile shoulders: mirrors HOYA.
  Creator of herself—her roots are packed tightly and run deep.
Suffering with space, they thrive in the crush of living density.
     Brazen legs spun through the soil of days—
              my roots are there as well.
    Once, the hairs of her thigh bit those of my hands.
We did not touch—clearly—
     though we embraced for two handfuls of glassy minutes.
HOYA spreads its spine,
        parabolic,
          its flesh quartered in all ways—and drawn to all rooms.
    Her feminine back worked so easily into the shape of a constellation yet named:
[Pins of sweat—minuscule stars.]
         I shall christen it surrender.
     Thrush of hair, rasping from the crown of a head,
like HOYA, illuminates—
        scouring the spring breeze for those particulates of life
        caught in the entanglement of chestnut web.
        She settles into the Earth.
        Soil moves for her.
  Looking—I envy its concern for the body.
Their fingers mimic, fingers dance—interlaced branches.
  like marrow and bone, one among the other.
Oppositional and pure: one bares its vulnerability, the other clasps...
              hiding the lines of its most
    naked organs—gazing—covets being gazed.
Lips part imperceptibly,
     breath escapes unnoticeably,
       hips twist gently,
         legs tow worlds to their bellies—languidly:
           hair trailing in the wake of their days.
    Without one, I cannot love the other. And with both, I cannot love either.

I had an odd dream—
it was a dream composite—
six dreams in one.
Many things happened.
In one, however, was you.
And we stood face to face.
Nose tip to nose tip.
Our mouths a crevasse—groaning, empty.
You smiled warmly and stood so effortlessly still.
And I felt anxious.
I read a poem out loud,
Felt it echo throughout empty space.
You did not move.
But you smiled warmly.
I kept reading poems.
I read my poems,
The poems of past poets,
The poems of future poets
        (stuttered in fragments).
You said nothing.
Waxy smile unmoving.
Then I read your poem.
I read it how I thought it should be read.
And you scowled.
And my anxiety melted.
Taking your hand, which was soft and muscular,
        I put it around my throat.
You squeezed.
You squeezed and smiled that waxy smile.
Your eyes were a rubbed brown—
        the rubbed brown of oil seeping through a fine sand.
And then the dream ended
And I went to the next dream.
And the next.

I awoke feeling the constriction

        of that soft hand.

I didn't sleep well.

Yesterday—there were

      eyes in the forest of night.

They reflected the eye of my torch.

      I longed to glide into the woods and grab what it was,

      but I did not.

Today, there was fur cast in the net of trees.

Something died in the woods last night.

I feel the woods around our home are so full of life and death.

      It is an electric pulse—the odd feeling of

longing for this unshattered wild, inside the house,

when there is such an

                unshattered

                        wild outside.

Exile

Entombed within a knit green afghan—

Spring morning filtered into lines

on the exile of Ovid in the deep barren recesses

of the "barbarian wastes"—   outer skirts of the Roman empire.

The story gelled with the predilection of attempting

to stew logic into the ombre of desolation

that acutely presents its body in daily life.

Never desolation of the dismayed senses,

but desolation in what is lived as eternal periods

of exposure to vacuum, vacuum of stimuli

Followed by rattling bursts of satisfying immersion in life.

And so it came to be, that at 6 am Ovid threw unto the skies

His hoarse voice—whilst clutching within his worn fingers

a child and an egg—for once more

to be able to feel life in the open wild,

and I was struck that this was how you come to me.

Wantonly to the aggrieved soul—sporadic bursts of feeling among

The torrential deluge of living: purely and simply.

. Post Script .

I do not know if you think of me
In such ways—
Or think of me at all.

i.

Disheveled morning mind—thinks:

Is a heart a heart,
when it is in the psalm of your hands,

or smouldering on a plate?
Or is it then,

Just a flesh to be consumed,
            or tipped aside.

A heart perhaps, becomes only a heart
when it gives life to whatever it constricts.

Is there still an anatomy as we can perceive,
But only in physicality?

The soothsayers, a thousand summers past,
Understood—that the raised bloody
            heart,

Could be the only piece of body
To appease the listless imposter gods.

ii.

            Post-coffee—

the spring is more welcome.

And post-bagel, the lilac marries gently

            to the pigs blood.

Copper tributary, flesh provides—and the

            sunrise scratched on gesso backs

Feels more alive. Did you know

            that oil is the death of a million

§

Bodies—last breaths encased in particulate

      black. And our magic

Has made it clear—and now, it sits upon

      the ledge of the Earth,

And resurrected, draws the long breath.

What would you do, to wake when all

      you knew is dust—and all you know

      Is before you?

iii.

      Grandfather—was seventy six:

Twenty seven thousand seven hundred and forty
Days alive. And now—
Roughly, two thousand nine hundred and twenty days gone.
When seventy six years of death have passed
The infinite memories spawned during his life,
Will have been balanced by the infinite emptiness of
      his absence.

There are warm nights—where I compress my love
For him, and send it out into the voiceless space:
Nothing has ever returned.
      A person, when they expire—does not live on.
I am sure, they collapse upon themselves, and begin
The long journey of reclaiming all that they perspired.
And in seventy six years—grandfather will have

      inhaled every breath he let slip.

And truly, there will be an emptiness where he once sat.

iv.

Three times   to be banished from the maternity ward,
Three times   to slither back—

      tunneling ferociously to the wailing ward,

§

With a cannibalistic veracity of a junkie in heat.
It's those sacks,
        the placentas you see: those juicy ripe plums ripped
        from the heavily heaving wombs.
The fragrant aromatics of former tombs—baptised in salt dew,
        where indents are perfectly laid: footprints for tongues
        To curl and lie among.
For tongues to curl and heave within—their bodies
        Against the shedding salt lick leather
        of a mother's deepest love.

Three times   to be banished from their kingdom of doors—
Three times   to slither back—

        every time have I returned, to ravish the keys left
Longing in the bins, left dangling from the locks of home.

.

She carries stigmata on the lips after sex—
        as she rests
The red currents of life spill forward,
        towards the end of
Satin sheets, run rivulets of sacrifice.
        Beautiful viscera;
        Beautiful bones;
        Beautiful anemic skin;
One must cup gently the handfuls of rare wine—
        must raise it delicately to the mouth.
Every drop of christened juice, crushed from
        grapes of birth,
        Must be savoured.

There lies a sense of heft in being—
        the heavy imposter sloughed across the chest.

For thirty-six Sunday summer mornings—
        A pound of history weighed upon the chest.

Have brows ever perceived drops upon their fine hairs—
        limbs felt as if merely swimming among the days,

running hands through the flotsam grown in the air—
        that floats on the surface of the days.

It is like the eroded crusts of ambergris—
        The concentrated regurgitation of something unborn;

Living far below the filtered fingers of light, in unmolested depths.
        Where to some, it reeks as would their guilt—reborn.

And to others—it is perfume.

        A ingot of beauty, that is revealed only by its longing to be purified—

        to be refined into a distilled and fragrant truth.

The grama is slain; let the severed heads lie—

Heads of kings and queens,

Halves of wholes—hearts and livers left

Seeded in the sod. Perhaps, their heads shall

      grow anew, to gaze

As they raise upon the heads of old selves

      which gently ripen at their feet.

This is the thinking of the world. Heads deposed

Are seeds for the fruits of future revolutions.

When the act is done—and the blade is sheathed—

Let them sleep where they have been laid—let them spy,

The last soft light—dew drip upon the fresh apple leaves.

Drooping, their emancipated necks float upon the breeze,

      and settle as freed feed

For the coming splendors of spring—their shoots

      ascending in praise to the endless gardens of flayed suns.

I Am the Voice of the Colossus [Creation]

Stained yellow smoker's teeth rattle much like those stacked in the tomb;

Some two thousand years of stale air with a donned wreath of good musky black mould

Would rot any gum, and soon after perishing, teeth would tile the floor,

And what precious jewels and gold were laid could not raise those teeth to beauty.

This made what was a disheveled place to lay the dead—with head room

Barely enough always grazing the cap of dead skin on that nightly

Jerking awake—seem eloquently upper class: a silk purse of mingling decomposition.

And the smoker's room in the one bedroom apartment off of main,

Behind the Sexpot Strip Club—mirrored a tomb. Friday nights there would

Be the ringing of Mahler, and the scratching of feet, and the shuffle of the

Vibrato hum resonating off every turned on light, and the grinding microwave

Heating another dinner for one—for the girlfriend cooked out on the sofa. Elderly

Eternal alcoholics don't eat, they subsist on the particles of person in air, the

Flecks of faces floating freely on the breeze. Inhaling lung after lung of

Glittering human liquefaction—and washed over by tides of almost ethanol, they are

vaporous spirits, shamanic undoings—that make wide berths of brave men, and close
        docks

Of soft women. And it is in both tombs, where both the dead lie—sun

Filtering to nothing, painting bands on the Jupiter gut of raging gas storms—that they

come to life. On Saturday mornings, behind heavy set curtains, can be heard the heavy

Set voice of the colossus: creation—massive and wakening—reaching for the button that

Builds the day. And in one press—the gutters tremble—and where the world and others

Sleep, here, creaking through the floors comes the god of subsistence existence—gathering

Precious empty vessels, to twist once more into life.

Figs—the favoured child of widows' seams—
moreish, of delicate touch,

with a nuanced nectar, whisperingly saccharine;
both versatile, and lush to the eye—its

skin textured just so—
Could be compared to the undeniable

seduction of the pink thighs of a
Of a woman waylaid in baths of steam.

Attended to—both, they part their frangible
legs, fans of limp flesh, gaping, mouths with a thousand

Seeded teeth—and there, glistens
the water of their cut throats.

And ripeness is an adolescence lost to weary
Age—the tender green hairless youth,

And taboo joinery under the stiff skirted leather
Of unsullied hides are mottled by the

relentless whips of nights and days.
And adolescence descends the crescent tongue

of hours—the end certain, consumed
Within the guts of the savouring many.

The dog whistle of their death is
Is rendered by the twisting canals of

of civilization—and man will toss
The craggy mountain cliffs, cross thistle

barefooted and bloody,
And suffer the banal tedium of scoured sand

to shelter, sleep, and bathe
In the deprivation of senses with the egg

With mauve yolks of sweet blood within the hand.
The packs of hounds, are two legged and dancing,

by firelight, and moonlight—daylight, and no light,
dancing—to celebrate the labour of

The spring Earth. And sacrificial, the official
Priests toss child upon child to the plate,

And knives honed of god stones,
honed on the doors and floors and walls

§

Of famished homes, flay the unspeaking,
Molested backs of those eternal pods.

Never does a tear of hate run from rested
Mounds of the fresh harvest—

and it is a sweet sadness, spread under the soft
Air—altars of flowers buds, their petals

spread, and calling for your love.
Calling for your tongue's caress.

Sweet predators—for years knifed on years,
They have slit the soft achilles of your lineage:

Diluted, your mouth has teethed on
Chairs not bone, and has torn cloth—not flesh.

Tied to the posts of the doors of warm homes, and
Cool waters—you have grown dumb. Yet,

The wilds fester in the forests of your gut.
The thickened roux of old blood mars the cold

Polished wood morning floors, and at times
Those in flight are borne to the dirt earth.

Sweet predators—for years knifed on years
They have pulled the chord of your depression,

ringing the howl of resignation to the moon
And the cold brittle airs. Padded feet, padding

Upon hard walls—painting the respiration of ones
History. Bengal usurpers of the shaded palms prey

Lives in glints upon the shimmer of your hawk eyes,
Judging the distant leaps and nearest shallows.

And against the furtive whip, which cracks at dawn,
Calls to prayer the hunter— and you are gone.

Sweet predators—for years knifed on years
you have wished to kill, and leave, and kill again—

Not for the rumble of chastised limbs—nor humble sermons
Of the famished wild thing. It is the bloodlust

Gifted to every generation. Inkling of terrible thirsts—
None will see, but me, your true intentions, transparent whims.

Where once, I have seen you wish to devour the newborn
Rendition of a beautiful winged king.

And yet, bound to the hardened fields which surround,
You are forced into service at the fattened feet of me.

About the Author

D. Mars Yuvarajan is a New Zealand poet. Mars was born in the United Kingdom and adopted New Zealand as his home in 1995. It was here among its expansive landscape that he honed his passion for poetry. Mars holds a Masters Degree in Poetry and has spent years as both an engineer, and then a Naval Officer before focusing purely on his literature. He now resides in the United States, and can be found in the hills of New Hampshire when not travelling the world to seek inspiration for his writings.